The author has always had a passion for writing. In the last years of high school, M. Maya signed to creative writing classes and won the annual poetry contest. Although her career took a different path, focusing on travelling and hospitality, she has always found time for "playing with words" as she likes to describe it.

In recent years M. Maya completed the diploma online "Freelance and Travel Writing" by the London School of Journalism and started freelancing for online publications. Having found her voice back as a writer, the author gained the confidence to start writing poetry again, this time in a foreign language.

In loving memory of my mum who inspires me every day.

M. Maya

ALL THE THINGS THAT CHANGE US

AUSTIN MACAULEY PUBLISHERS™
LONDON • CAMBRIDGE • NEW YORK • SHARJAH

ISBN – 9789948787365 – (Paperback)
ISBN – 9789948787372 – (E-Book)

Application Number: MC-10-01-7694375
Age Classification: E

First Published 2023
AUSTIN MACAULEY PUBLISHERS FZE
Sharjah Publishing City
P.O Box [519201]
Sharjah, UAE

www.austinmacauley.ae
+971 655 95 202

Thank you to friends and family close and afar.

Thank you to all the experiences and people that got me here today and made *All the Things That Change us*.

At the end of the journey
I don't want to be made
Of the love letters
I've never sent you.

I've seen you hiding,
From the corner of my eye.
You remind me of
The days
I cried too much,
I tried too hard,
I lived too fast.

He was a small boy
With big dreams.
The struggle arrived
When he became a big boy
With very small dreams.

She was like a modern version of Cinderella
On the way back from the bar
In a summer night.
Soul drowned on cheap tequila
Because she took it all too far.

I invented endless conversations
In a secret room of my mind.
I stripped him smoothly
And rubbed his back with my words.
I wasn't ready to let go.

We are meant to meet again
Like the sun is meant to set.
And the words are meant to flow
like the tides are meant to grow.
And my love will not get old.
And my hope is meant to stay.
We are meant to meet again.
Like the sun is meant to set.
And my soul is meant to break
So I can finally fly and forget.

I want to touch you softly
With my words
And make love to you
With my brain
While I take you for a late-night drive
In the deepness of my soul.

I write so one day we both remember,
Where there is love,
It gets never cold.
I write so you can see my mind and soul
And at the same time
I kiss yours.
I write so I can move you
with the power of my ever-
Silent words.
I write because it gives me all,
Asking for nothing in return.
I write because you
Might be struggling,
And I would love to bring you hope.

He was the salt to my tequila,
Also the lemon to my open wounds.

In the mood for
Adventure-filled days,
Roasting marshmallows
Under the stars,
Playing silly songs
On my guitar
Around a bonfire.
In the mood for life!

In the mood for
Vanilla-scented candles,
Bubble baths,
Soft words
And warm cuddles.
In the mood for you.

In the mood for
Cheap box wine,
Chocolate ice-cream
And rotten pyjamas.
Not in the mood for you.

I have known you
A whole antique winter.
I am now scared
my summers
will start to fade.

I believe in breakups
That mess you up.
In make-ups
That mess you up even more.
I believe in sex without love.
Oh, and I nearly forgot,
I believe in sweet old love.

She mastered the art
Of turning mistakes
Into lessons.
Regrets into remakes.
Dark into bright.
She was not intelligent,
But she was smart.

He wants to be free.
Open the window
And help him fly.
He will ask to return.
Your window may still be open
But he will be flying back
With broken wings.

We fear for the change
And long for the past.
Sad enough,
We don't fear not to change
While waiting to expire.

I've caught my own echo
Mumbling words by mistake.
I then remembered
How lonely it can get up there
In my head.

The biggest betrayal was
Her lips
Crying his name
While kissing yours.

I travelled through your light
Connected to your soul
Got lost a thousand miles
Came back kissing stars.
I travelled through your light
Wrote verses a midnight
Got lost a thousand miles
Went back bringing blue skies.
I travelled through your light
Went diving into old minds
Got lost a thousand miles.
I was reborn to rewrite.

Stealing my dreams
And still
In my dreams.
Every day.
Every moon.
Every night.
Every breath.
I relive his smell,
His tone,
His peace.
I would draw him in my mind again,
Again and again.
Every curve.
Every turn.
Every swell.
Every breath.
Still.

In the windy winter days,
I will always keep a gust of hope.
With my feathers wet and my soul warm,
I look forward to your return.

Aching inside.
Itching to leave.
Willing to change.
Longing to belong.
Needing to breathe.
And I met you.
And I was no longer
Aching,
Itching,
Willing,
Longing,
Needing.
I was just living.

Baby! Did you call me?
I guess it's lonely
In your pants
Tonight.

And in these hidden places
Where you go to sob and weep,
I will be still standing
To remind you:
You are enough.
When you feel your legs like jelly
And your soul tearing apart,
I will be still standing
To remind you:
You are enough.
Once the pain has left your body
And you get ready to fly,
I will be there standing
To remind you:
Don't look back.

It's about time.
It's about the time you wasted second-guessing,
Stressing,
Overthinking,
Regretting
And worrying about all the things
You can't control.
It's about that one day,
That one hour,
That one minute,
That one extra second that could have changed it all.
It's about the time we think we have
And then we haven't.
It's about living,
Loving
And knowing when to leave.
It's all about time.
It's about now.

We were a combination
Of hard sarcasm,
Wild nights,
Jokes taken too far.
We were fire.
We would fight and make up
With the same passion
As the first-timers.
We were madness.
We were the deep talkers,
The secret lovers
And the moonlight dancers.
We were life.
We were the question marks,
The silences for answers
And the not taking it too serious.
We were perfect in my eyes.

I wish I could look at you
The way I used to
Look at him
No matter what.

He reminded me of a certain somewhere
With cloudy mornings
But bright sunny days.
The perfect touch of heat
And a tumultuous storm from time to time,
Just to keep me grounded
And don't let me forget
That not every day can be made of sunshine.

She will always be my weakness,
My fear,
My regret.
My most painful memory.
And I will do it all over again
Just to see her wanting more,
Craving more,
Hurting more,
While I walk away.

I like my words
Like I like my coffee:
Strong,
Earthy
And with a mellow
Aftertaste.

Stuck inside the four cold walls,
Locked down,
Deprived.
There are worse things.
We write.
We read.
We sip.
We smile.
We drink some more.
We rewrite.
We smile.
And at the end of the evening,
We are a little bit drunker
And a little more in love.

Yeah, I wish!
And I am so awfully mad!
It's not on you,
Or on me,
Or anyone.
It's on life!

I like to sit there,
On the edge.
Feeling every breath.
Talking to the blue.
Playing with the breeze.
Touching every drop.
And be,
And feel
And exist.
Living in the now.

In a world where love is
Based on likes,
Where relationships end with an unfollow.
Where a date starts with a click,
And there's plenty of fish in the sea,
Yet, everybody seems lonely to me.
Put your phone away
And be committed to fall back in love
With yourself.

Music is you and I
Under a sky full of falling stars.
Art is the way you look away
While you are making up a lie.
Pain is the way I smile
Deep down breaking inside.
Poetry is what you make me feel,
Even when things get hard.

45

I've lost my cool,
My temper,
My voice
That's all far gone.
I've lost the breadcrumbs
Marking my way home.

You came to visit me last night,
In blue.
I've got the biggest hug from you,
In blue.
I've been immerse ever since
In a daydream blues.
Your voice is still harsh,
Your hands the softest of the soft.
I now know; it will all be fine.
Thank you for visiting last night,
In blue.
I do not want to wake up.

With the last autumn rain,
The storm shifted his thoughts.
His heart warmed up as the wind changed.
He was no longer there, waiting.
He was somewhere else, surviving.

I wish you the best.
I wish you to fall in love again.
I wish you to fall in love with life,
With cotton candy sunsets,
With the smell of freshly brewed coffee,
With a hug so tight you struggle to breathe,
Yet, you can't let go.
I wish you to fall hard for stimulating conversations
With the moon
Somewhere on a roof at midnight.
I wish you to fall deep for every inch of your body
And every sharp corner of your soul.

I sat by the fire,
Wrapped up in a blanket
Thick socks as my armour.
Waiting, waiting and waiting.
I knew with the spring
His colours will again flourish.
Sorry darling, I am more of a summer girl.

There is night-blind,
Colour blind,
Temporary-blind
And permanent irreversible lust-blind.
Honey, you don't love him.

All she ever wanted were
More sunsets,
More puppies,
More avocadoes on toast
A best Friend she could blindly trust,
Someone she could call Home.

I've stop dragging my feet through the floor.
I wasn't carrying it all anymore.
Learning to go with the flow.
My usual was no longer tiptoe.
My guard was down,
Mood on point.
I caught a glimpse of him,
Cocky thing leaning on the door.
Oh, boy!
Here we go.

There is a magic place on Earth,
Where the mind sets free,
Where time doesn't matter,
Where the sound is made of an exquisite silence.
That place is in your soul.

54

Self-respect holds you,
While self-esteem enhances you
For self-love to strengthen you.
Self-worth will challenge you
So self-confidence can empower you
And all of them will guide you.

Lost in our memories
Is my favourite place to be.

Thank you